Boston
MEDIA MAKERS

Connecting People Who Benefit from Knowing Each Other

Photos by Steve Garfield, Jeff Cutler and Alecia Jean Orsini Lebeda. Book design by J. Bruce Jones.

Published by Boston Media Makers • https://bostonmediamakers.com © Copyright Steve Garfield 2018

Thanks to Doyle's Café for hosting our meetings. Voted Boston's Best Pub, Doyle's is also a historic landmark in Jamaica Plain offering New England's largest selection of draft beer, and the first home of Sam Adams Beer. 3484 Washington Street, Jamaica Plain, MA 02130 | Phone: (617) 524-2345 https://www.doylescafeboston.com office.doyles@gmail.com

Boston Media Makers

Hosted by Steve Garfield.

Boston Media Makers is a monthly meet-up for media enthusiasts in the Greater Boston Area. We are social media enthusiasts, filmmakers, journalists, web geeks, technologists, designers, artists, entrepreneurs, and people just wanting to learn more about making and distributing media online. Come talk shop and share current projects. The guest presenter is YOU. Everyone gets three minutes to share, pitch, promote, or ask questions.
We learn, get inspired, and collaborate.

I was at a meeting of over 300 people at MIT and there was a Q & A session during the meeting. One person got up from CBS New York. I thought, "I'd like to meet that person. Then I thought, I'd like to meet every other person at this meeting, they are probably interesting too." Then I started Boston Media Makers so every person at the meeting could meet every other person.

This meeting started out with people who were working with audio and video on the web but over the years it has expanded to include podcasters, video bloggers, filmmakers, artists, actors, musicians, writers, programmers, news reporters, PR and social media people.
We help people GET SEEN.

What We Do

We gather around a big table and answer the questions
- What are you doing?
- What do you want to do?
- Do you need some help?
- You can ask questions too.
- Come with a prepared show and tell if you like.

https://bostonmediamakers.com

What are you doing?

What do you want to do?

Do you need some help?

You can ask questions too.

Come with a prepared
show and tell if you like.

Results for #bmm

Tweets Top / All / People you follow

Steve Garfield @stevegarfield
Fear the Bear. **#bmm** @ Doyle's Cafe
instagram.com/p/aDyemyhCs3/
📍 from Boston, MA   7m

Steve Garfield @stevegarfield
@bruceKgarber See you soon. Good to hear the A/C is on. **#bmm**
In reply to Bruce Garber   26m
💬 View conversation

Joseph Silva @joeyswirled
Yo @stevegarfield et al, though I'll be on **#BayonneBridge** to SI
during the meeting I'm attending **#BMM** in spirit. **#Boston**
Favorited by Steve Garfield   43m
📍 from Bayonne, NJ

Havok @Droan_SCW
@Supr_Niccuh is **#BMM** the name of your song or something ?
💬 View conversation   56m

Bayard E.Kidd™ @DrKddd.Kidd
Oh the **#BMM** hash tag stands for black music month. I'm giving
artist who I like and a brief bio of them. Check em out.
Expand   1h

Bayard E.Kidd™ @DrKddd.Kidd
Jerome Najee Rasheed known professionally as Najee, is an
American smooth jazz saxophonist and flautist. **#BMM**
Expand   1h

Steve Garfield @stevegarfield
Driving to Boston Media M...
walkers. #bmm

Breakfast is pretty good too.